D0437876

An easy and enjoyable introduction to one of
America's greatest presidents and heroes.

—*Tom Schwartz*
Illinois State Historian

Gordon Leidner provides readers with a
toothsome smorgasboard of Abraham Lincoln's
wit and wisdom. This volume is an excellent
introduction to the Great Emancipator's
humanity, philosophy, humor, and eloquence. To
supplement Lincoln's own memorable words,
Leidner adds judicious comments by such
eminent figures as Frederick Douglass, Theodore
Roosevelt, and Booker T. Washington.

—*Michael Burlingame*
Sadowski Professor of History Emeritus
Connecticut College

Abraham Lincoln had the God-given talent to
express himself in words that the people felt and
understood. [This] book enables readers to
sample and touch the greatness of Lincoln
through his letters, public papers, and speeches.

—*Edwin C. Bearss*
Historian Emeritus, National Park Service

ABRAHAM LINCOLN

Quotes, Quips, AND *Speeches*

GORDON LEIDNER
Editor

CUMBERLAND HOUSE
NASHVILLE, TENNESSEE

ABRAHAM LINCOLN: QUOTES, QUIPS, AND SPEECHES

PUBLISHED BY CUMBERLAND HOUSE PUBLISHING INC.

431 Harding Industrial Drive

Nashville, Tennessee 37211

Cover design by Gore Studio Inc., Nashville, Tennessee

Library of Congress Cataloging-in-Publication Data

Lincoln, Abraham, 1809–1865.

Abraham Lincoln : quotes, quips, and speeches / Gordon Leidner, editor.

p. cm.

Rev. ed. of: A commitment to honor : a unique portrait of Abraham Lincoln in his own words. Nashville, Tenn. : Rutledge Press, c2000.

Includes bibliographical references.

ISBN-13: 978-1-58182-677-7 (hardcover : alk. paper)

ISBN-10: 1-58182-677-X (hardcover : alk. paper)

1. Lincoln, Abraham, 1809–1865—Quotations. 2. Presidents—United
States—Quotations. 3. United States—Politics and government—Quotations, maxims, etc. 4. Conduct of life—Quotations, maxims, etc. I. Leidner, Gordon, 1954– II. Lincoln, Abraham, 1809–1865. Commitment to
honor. III. Title.

E457.99.L4 2009

973.7092—dc22   2008037639

Printed in the United States of America

2 3 4 5 6 7 8 9 10—12 11 10 09

In memory of my mother—
BETTY LEIDNER

Contents

Preface

AMERICANS HAVE been fascinated with Abraham Lincoln for more than a century. Our fascination with and respect for Lincoln is rooted in his legacy both as a preserver of the Union and as the Great Emancipator. We also esteem him as an embodiment of integrity, faith, generosity, and determination. He persevered and fought his way up to occupy the highest office of the land, doing so without benefit of wealth, advantage, or formal education. We value his state papers, speeches, and letters as eloquent testimonies of his statesmanship and striking character. Ever since Lincoln's death at the hands of an assassin, people have acknowledged that his life is an excellent example of what honesty, determination, and industry can accomplish under a democratic government.

My interest in Lincoln and the Civil War began during my childhood. I grew up in southern Illinois, where Lincoln lore is integral to local

history. In September 1858 Lincoln had honored
my hometown of Greenville with a visit in between his famous debate appointments with
Stephen A. Douglas at Freeport and Jonesboro.
Vandalia, a neighboring community, is the home
of the second state capitol and is where Lincoln
began his political career as a state representative
from Sangamon County. Vandalia has the added
distinction of being the city where Lincoln first
publicly declared the "injustice" of slavery.

My task in assembling this book of Lincoln
quotations primarily was to wade through moun-
tains of Lincoln material, distinguish the genuine
from the proverbial, and select the best of the
best. The quotes herein are taken from the
sources listed in the notes. I've made occasional
minor changes in punctuation and corrected mis-
spellings to improve readability.

Lincoln lived his life with a commitment to
honor, and in this book the admirable qualities
and virtues he embodied are examined in some
detail and through his words. Included in each of
the twelve chapters are observations of Lincoln by
some of the people who knew him best, validating
Lincoln's association with the discussed virtue.

My intention is to provide casual readers with short, reliable, and inspirational quotes from America's sixteenth president as well as a handful of excerpts from his most famous speeches. Think of this book as an inspirational and motivational guide on how to live life today, emulating the best qualities of perhaps our nation's greatest leader.

—Gordon Leidner

Biography

ABRAHAM LINCOLN was born near Hodgenville, Kentucky, on February 12, 1809. Raised in poverty by deeply religious parents, he had received less than a year of formal education by the time he turned twenty-one. He moved to New Salem, Illinois, in 1831 and continued his self-education there by borrowing books and teaching himself grammar, history, mathematics, and law.

Outgoing and ambitious, Lincoln was anxious to make his mark in politics. He was elected one of Sangamon County's Whig representatives to the Illinois state legislature in 1834. Vocally antislavery, served four consecutive terms as state legislator, during which time he was admitted to the state bar. He soon became one of the most respected attorneys in the region, known particularly for his honesty and influential manner with juries.

In 1842 Lincoln married Mary Todd, a well-educated woman of a notable Kentucky family.

They eventually had four sons, although only one survived to adulthood.

Lincoln served a term in Congress from 1847 to 1849. He then went into semiretirement from politics in order to concentrate on his law practice. The Kansas-Nebraska Act of 1854, allowing for the introduction of slavery into the new territories, enticed Lincoln to again seek political office. He joined the Republican Party in 1856 and ran for the U.S. Senate in 1858, generating an energetic moral argument against slavery in a series of debates with the incumbent Democrat, Stephen A. Douglas.

Lincoln lost the Senate race to Douglas but two years later, in 1860, was elected president. Subsequent to his election, eleven Southern states declared their independence from the Union. Although Lincoln knew that slavery was the underlying cause of the war, he realized that to declare a war against slavery would result in many of the Northern people's refusal to fight. When the South fired on Fort Sumter on April 12, 1860, Lincoln declared a war to preserve the Union and called the North to arms.

It was more than a year into the Civil War before Lincoln was finally able to add the elimination of slavery to the war's purposes. His Emancipation Proclamation, freeing the slaves of the rebelling Southern states, took effect on January 1, 1863. Through his personal leadership, the Thirteenth Amendment, which legally abolished slavery, was passed by Congress and sent to the states for ratification.

Subsequent Union victories at Gettysburg, Vicksburg, and Chattanooga soon had the Southern armies permanently on the defensive. Lincoln was reelected president in November 1864.

Lincoln's second inaugural address, delivered less than six weeks before his assassination, eloquently summed up his beliefs: the underlying cause of the war had been slavery; the war was God's just punishment on the nation for its failure to remove slavery from the land; and it was every American's duty not only to accept the elimination of slavery but to forgive his or her fellow man and pursue a "lasting peace" with all nations.

Lincoln was shot by John Wilkes Booth on April 14, 1865, and died the following day.

ABRAHAM LINCOLN

Quotes, Quips, AND *Speeches*

I

Leadership

BEFORE HE WAS ELECTED president in 1860, Lincoln had little formal education, no administrative training, and held only one term in a national office, as a congressman from Illinois. His only military experience had been a few weeks of service in the state militia during the Black Hawk War.

Many of the North's most powerful political leaders wanted to let the South secede. Lincoln, however, was committed to preserving the Union and made his every task subservient to this cause. Although it is significant that he successfully led the war effort, including hiring and firing generals and cabinet members until he found the people who could achieve this victory, his most important accomplishment probably was the continuous motivation of the public to support the cause in spite of the terrible losses incurred during the long years of war.

It was in the oath I took that I would, to the best of my ability, preserve, protect, and defend the Constitution of the United States. I could not take the office without taking the oath. Nor was it my view that I might take an oath to get power, and break the oath in using the power.[1]

I don't know but that God has created some one man great enough to comprehend the whole of this stupendous crisis and transaction from beginning to end, and endowed him with sufficient wisdom to manage and direct it. I confess I do not fully understand, and foresee it all. But I am placed here where I am obliged to the best of my poor ability to deal with it.[2]

I am decided; my course is fixed; my path is blazed. The Union and the Constitution shall be preserved and the laws enforced at every and at all hazards. I expect the people to sustain me. They have never yet forsaken any true man.[3]

In your hands, my dissatisfied fellow-countrymen, and not in mine, is the momentous issue of civil war. The government will not assail you. You can have no conflict without being yourselves the aggressors. You have no oath registered in heaven to destroy the government, while I shall have the most solemn one to "preserve, protect, and defend it."[4]

Neither let us be slandered from our duty by false accusations against us, nor frightened from it by menaces of destruction to the government, nor of dungeons to ourselves. Let us have faith that right makes might; and in that faith let us to the end dare to do our duty as we understand it.[5]

I attempt no compliment to my own sagacity. I claim not to have controlled events, but confess plainly that events have controlled me. Now, at the end of three years' struggle, the nation's condition is not what either party, or any man, devised or expected. God alone can claim it.[6]

*H*e would listen to everybody; he would hear everybody; but he rarely, if ever, asked for opinions. As a politician and as president, he arrived at all his conclusions from his own reflections, and when his opinion was once formed, he never doubted that it was right.[7]

Leonard Swett, close friend of Lincoln

Think nothing of me—take no thought for the political fate of any man whomsoever, but come back to the truths that are in the Declaration of Independence. . . . I charge you to drop every paltry and insignificant thought for any man's success. It is nothing; I am nothing; Judge Douglas [that is, Stephen A. Douglas] is nothing. But do not destroy that immortal emblem of Humanity—the Declaration of American Independence.[8]

The Union must be preserved, and hence, all indispensable means must be employed.[9]

Let there be no compromise on the question of extending slavery. If there be, all our labor is lost, and ere long, must be done again. The dangerous ground—that into which some of our friends have a hankering to run—is Popular Sovereignty. Have none of it. Stand firm.[10]

By general law, life and limb must be protected, yet often a limb must be amputated to save a life; but a life is never wisely given to save a limb. I felt that measures otherwise unconstitutional might become lawful by becoming indispensable to the preservation of the Constitution through the preservation of the nation. Right or wrong, I assumed this ground and now avow it.[11]

I have always thought that all men should be free; but if any should be slaves it should be first those who desire it for themselves, and secondly those who desire it for others. Whenever [I] hear any one, arguing for slavery I feel a strong impulse to see it tried on him personally.[12]

*I*n small and unimportant matters, Mr. Lincoln was so yielding that many thought his excessive amiability was born of weakness. But, in matters of vital importance, he was firm as a rock. Neither Congress nor his cabinet could, in the slightest degree, influence his action on great questions, against the convictions of his patriotic judgment.[13]

John B. Alley, congressman (R-MA) and friend of Lincoln

*I*f I were to try to read, much less answer, all the attacks made on me, this shop might as well be closed for any other business. I do the very best I know how—the very best I can; and I mean to keep doing so until the end. If the end brings me out all right, what is said against me won't amount to anything. If the end brings me out wrong, ten thousand angels swearing I was right would make no difference.[14]

With all his awkwardness of manner, and utter disregard of social conventionalities that seemed to invite familiarity, there was something about Abraham Lincoln that enforced respect. No man presumed on the apparent invitation to be other than respectful.[15]

Donn Piatt, soldier and journalist

While acting as their representative, I shall be governed by [the people's] will on all subjects upon which I have the means of knowing what their will is; and upon all others I shall do what my own judgment teaches me will best advance their interests.[16]

It is as much the duty of government to render prompt justice against itself, in favor of citizens, as it is to administer the same, between private individuals.[17]

*E*ven in [Lincoln's] freest moments one always felt the presence of a will and an intellectual power which maintained the ascendancy of the president. He never posed or put on airs or attempted to make any particular impression; but he was always conscious of his own ideas and purposes, even in his most unreserved moments.[18]

> *Charles A. Dana, assistant secretary of war in*
> *the Lincoln administration*

Towering genius disdains a beaten path.[19]

2

Honesty

LINCOLN EARNED THE NICKNAME "Honest Abe" as a young man working as a store clerk. It is recorded that if he realized he had accidentally shortchanged a customer a few pennies, he thought nothing of closing up the shop and walking several miles to deliver the correct change. Recognizing Lincoln's honesty, people were soon asking him to act as judge or referee at various events. He became a popular arbiter of wrestling matches, horse races, and petty squabbles.

Whether as a clerk in a country store, representative in the state legislature, or lawyer in court, Lincoln dealt honestly with everyone. Throughout his entire career in politics and public service, he was extremely proud of his reputation and took great care to justify the Honest Abe sobriquet.

*O*n the underlying principles of truth and justice his will was as firm as steel and as tenacious as iron.[1]

William Herndon, law partner and close friend of Lincoln

I planted myself upon the truth and the truth only, so far as I knew it, or could be brought to know it.[2]

I have always wanted to deal with everyone I meet candidly and honestly. If I have made any assertion not warranted by facts, and it is pointed out to me, I will withdraw it cheerfully.[3]

I made a point of honor and conscience in all things to stick to my word, especially if others had been induced to act on it.[4]

Resolve to be honest at all events; and if in your judgment you cannot be an honest lawyer, resolve to be honest without being a lawyer. Choose some other occupation, rather than one in the choosing of which you do, in advance, consent to be a knave.[5]

I shall have my hands full. He is the strong man of his party—full of wit, facts, dates—and the best stump speaker, with his droll ways and dry jokes, in the West. He is as honest as he is shrewd, and if I beat him my victory will be hardly won.[6]

> *Sen. Stephen A. Douglas, upon hearing that*
> *Lincoln would be his opponent in Illinois's*
> *1858 U.S. Senate race*

I wish at all times in no way to practice any fraud upon the House or the committee, and I also desire to do nothing which may be very disagreeable to any of the members [of Congress].[7]

I don't want to be unjustly accused of dealing illiberally or unfairly with an adversary, either in court, or in a political canvass, or anywhere else. I would despise myself if I supposed myself ready to deal less liberally with an adversary than I was willing to be treated myself.[8]

I am glad of all the support I can get anywhere, if I can get it without practicing any deception to obtain it.[9]

I do not state a thing and say I know it when I do not. . . . I mean to put a case no stronger than the truth will allow.[10]

Mr. Lincoln . . . is almost monomaniac on the subject of honesty.[11]

*Mary Todd Lincoln, writing to a friend about
her husband's insistence on truthfulness*

*H*is moral character stands among us here without reproach or blemish. I have known him for twenty years, and latterly as circumstances have made him more prominent I have become well acquainted with him, and have watched the course of public opinion in these parts, both among his friends and his foes. . . . Abraham Lincoln has been here all the time, consulting and consulted by all classes, all parties, and on all subjects of political interest, with men of every degree of corruption and yet I have never heard even an enemy accuse him of intentional dishonesty or corruption. . . . He has stood before the community here the man of uncorrupted if not incorruptible integrity, and to be able to say that of any man who has mingled as freely with Illinois politics and politicians as Mr. Lincoln has is glory enough for one man.[12]

Rev. Albert Hale, pastor of the Second
Presbyterian Church of Springfield

If it is decreed that I should go down because of this speech, then let me go down linked to the truth—let me die in the advocacy of what is just and right.[13]

Stand with anybody that stands right. Stand with him while he is right, and part with him when he goes wrong.[14]

I have never tried to conceal my opinions, nor tried to deceive anyone in reference to them.[15]

You must remember that some things legally right are not morally right.[16]

*M*r. Lincoln's judgment was final in all that region of the country. People relied implicitly upon his honesty, integrity, and impartiality.[17]

> *Robert B. Rutledge, resident of New Salem when Lincoln lived there*

Truth is generally the best vindication against slander.[18]

In very truth he [that is, a deceased associate] was the noblest work of God—an honest man.[19]

*T*he framework for [Lincoln's] mental and moral being was honesty, and a wrong cause was poorly defended by him.[20]

> *Judge David Douglas, in whose court Lincoln practiced law for fourteen years*

You have nominated a very able and very honest man.[21]

> *Stephen A. Douglas, upon hearing that the*
> *1860 Republican Convention had nominated*
> *Lincoln for the presidency*

Every man is said to have his peculiar ambition. Whether it be true or not, I can say, for one, that I have no other so great as that of being truly esteemed of my fellow-men, by rendering myself worthy of their esteem. How far I shall succeed in gratifying this ambition is yet to be developed. I am young, and unknown to many of you. I was born, and have ever remained, in the most humble walks of life. I have no wealthy or popular relations or friends to recommend me. My case is thrown exclusively upon the independent voters of the county; and, if elected, they will have conferred a favor upon me for which I shall be unremitting in my labors to compensate. But, if the good people in their wisdom shall see fit to keep me in the background, I have been too familiar with disappointments to be very much chagrined.[22]

3

Faith

HISTORIANS FREQUENTLY DEBATE LINCOLN'S
faith. Some say Lincoln was an unbeliever, or at
least a skeptic, of Christianity. Many say he was a
"deeply religious" man who sought God's guid-
ance daily.

Lincoln never formally joined a church, but
he knew the Bible very well. He memorized a
great deal of Scripture and could quote it better
than many ministers of the gospel. Even though
Lincoln went through a period of skepticism as
a young man, his confidence in the Bible grew
significantly as he matured and survived life's
hardships. By the time he had become president, Lincoln was a man of deep faith.

As president, Lincoln frequently discussed his
dependence on God, acknowledging that his most
earnest prayer was to determine the Lord's will so
that he could follow it.

Whatever shall appear to be God's will I will do.[1]

The will of God prevails. In great contests each party claims to act in accordance with the will of God. Both may be, and one must be, wrong. God cannot be for and against the same thing at the same time. In the present civil war it is quite possible that God's purpose is something different from the purpose of either party; and yet the human instrumentalities, working just as they do, are of the best adaptation to effect his purpose. I am almost ready to say that this is probably true; that God wills this contest, and wills that it shall not end yet.[2]

If we do right God will be with us, and if God is with us we cannot fail.[3]

There is no contending against the Will of God; but still there is some difficulty in ascertaining, and applying it, to particular cases.[4]

Amid the greatest difficulties of my Administration, when I could not see any other resort, I would place my whole reliance in God, knowing that all would go well, and that He would decide for the right.[5]

I am not at all concerned about that [that is, God's being on the Northern side in the war], for I know the Lord is always on the side of the right. But it is my constant anxiety and prayer that I and this nation should be on *the Lord's* side.[6]

He never joined a Church; but still, as I believe, he was a religious man by nature.[7]
    Mary Todd Lincoln

Take all of this Book [that is, the Bible] upon reason that you can and the balance on faith, and you will live and die a happier and better man.[8]

*A*s [Lincoln] became involved in matters of
the greatest importance, full of great responsibility and great doubt, a feeling of religious rev-
erence, a belief in God and his justice and
overruling power increased with him. . . . He
believed in the great laws of truth, and the rigid
discharge of duty, his accountability to God, the
ultimate triumph of the right and the overthrow of wrong. If his religion were to be
judged by the lines and rules of Church creeds,
he would fall far short of the standard; but if by
the higher rule of purity of conduct, of honesty
of motive, of unyielding fidelity to the right,
and acknowledging God as the supreme ruler,
then he filled all the requirements of true devotion, and his whole life was a life of love to God,
and love of his neighbor as of himself.[9]

Leonard Swett, close friend of Lincoln

That I am not a member of any Christian
church is true; but I have never denied the truth
of the Scriptures.[10]

We are indeed going through a trial—a fiery trial. In the very responsible position in which I happen to be placed, being a humble instrument in the hands of our Heavenly Father, as I am, and as we all are, to work out His great purposes, I have desired that all my works and acts may be according to His will, and that it might be so, I have sought His aid—but if after endeavoring to do my best in the light which He affords me, I find my efforts fail, I must believe that for some purpose unknown to me, He wills it otherwise.[11]

Our political problem now is "Can we, as a nation, continue together permanently—forever—half slave, and half free?" The problem is too mighty for me. May God, in his mercy, superintend the solution.[12]

I made a solemn vow before God, that if General [Robert E.] Lee was driven back from Pennsylvania I would crown the results by the declaration of freedom to the slaves.[13]

The purposes of the Almighty are perfect, and must prevail, though we erring mortals may fail to accurately perceive them in advance. We hoped for a happy termination of this terrible war long before this; but God knows best, and has ruled otherwise. We shall yet acknowledge His wisdom, and our own error therein. Meanwhile we must work earnestly in the best lights He gives us, trusting that so working still conduces to the great ends He ordains. Surely He intends some great good to follow this mighty convulsion, which no mortal could make, and no mortal could stay.[14]

It is most cheering and encouraging for me to know that in the efforts which I have made and am making for the restoration of a righteous peace to our country, I am upheld and sustained by the good wishes and prayers of God's people. No one is more deeply than myself aware that without His favor our highest wisdom is but as foolishness and that our most strenuous efforts would avail nothing in the shadow of His displeasure.[15]

It is the duty of nations as well as of men to own
their dependence upon the overruling power of
God; to confess their sins and transgressions, in
humble sorrow, yet with assured hope that genuine repentance will lead to mercy and pardon;
and to recognize the sublime truth, announced
in the Holy Scriptures and proven by all history,
that those nations only are blessed whose God is
the Lord. . . .

We have been preserved, these many years, in
peace and prosperity. We have grown in numbers, wealth, and power as no other nation has
ever grown; but we have forgotten God. We have
forgotten the gracious hand which has preserved
us in peace, and multiplied and enriched and
strengthened us; and we have vainly imagined, in
the deceitfulness of our hearts, that all these
blessings were produced by some superior wisdom and virtue of our own. Intoxicated with
unbroken success, we have become too self-
sufficient to feel the necessity of redeeming and
preserving grace, too proud to pray to the God
that made us. . . .

It behooves us, then, to humble ourselves before the offended Power, to confess our national
sins, and to pray for clemency and forgiveness.[16]

From Lincoln's proclamation appointing a
National Fast Day, March 30, 1863

I should be the most presumptuous blockhead
upon this footstool if I for one day thought that I
should discharge the duties which have come
upon me, since I came to this place, without the
aid and enlightenment of One who is stronger
and wiser than all others.[17]

In regards to this great Book [the Bible], I have
but to say, it is the best gift God has given to
men. All the good Savior gave to this world was
communicated through this Book. But for it we
could not know right from wrong. All things
most desirable for man's welfare, here and hereafter, are to be found portrayed in it.[18]

On principle I dislike an oath which requires a man to swear he has not done wrong. It rejects the Christian principle of forgiveness on terms of repentance. I think it is enough if the man does no wrong hereafter.[19]

4

The People

LINCOLN HAD TREMENDOUS FAITH in people. Having grown up in the midwestern wilderness, he had watched his family and neighbors overcome hardships typical of pioneers in the early nineteenth century. He believed that Americans were the most intelligent, industrious, and resourceful people in the world. Convinced that their character was reflected in the democratic government they had formed, he believed that as long as the people retained "their virtue and vigilance," they would never be successfully misled by corrupt politicians or sophists.

Lincoln believed in people because he knew them. One of his greatest qualities as a leader was his ability to recognize the strengths and weaknesses of others and then use each individual effectively for the benefit of the nation.

I think of the whole people of this nation; they will ever do well if well done by.[1]

The people will save their government if the government itself will do its part only indifferently well.[2]

Why should there not be a patient confidence in the ultimate justice of the people? Is there any better or equal hope in the world?[3]

I appeal to you [the people] again to constantly bear in mind that not with politicians, not with Presidents, not with office-seekers, but with you is the question, "Shall the Union, shall the liberties of this country, be preserved to the latest generations?"[4]

In leaving the people's business in their hands, we cannot be wrong.[5]

At what point then is the approach of danger to be expected? I answer, if it ever reach us it must spring up amongst us; it cannot come from abroad. If destruction be our lot we must ourselves be its author and finisher. As a nation of freemen we must live through all time or die by suicide.[6]

This is essentially a people's contest. On the side of the Union it is a struggle for maintaining in the world that form and substance of government whose leading object is to elevate the condition of men—to lift artificial weights from all shoulders; to clear the paths of laudable pursuit for all; to afford all an unfettered start, and a fair chance in the race of life. . . . I am most happy to believe that the plain people understand and appreciate this.[7]

The integrity of our country and the stability of our government mainly depend . . . on the loyalty, virtue, patriotism, and intelligence of the American people.[8]

*H*e [Lincoln] prized the suggestions of the unsophisticated people more than what was called statecraft or political wisdom. He really believed that the voice of the people in our emergency was [the] next thing to the voice of God.[9]

Joseph Gillespie, longtime friend and legal associate of Lincoln

It is, fellow-citizens, for the whole American people, and not for one single man alone, to advance the great cause of the Union and the Constitution. And in a country like this, where every man bears on his face the marks of intelligence, where every man's clothing, if I may so speak, shows signs of comfort, and every dwelling signs of happiness and contentment, where schools and churches abound on every side, the Union can never be in danger.[10]

Encompassed by vast difficulties as I am, nothing shall be wanting my part, if sustained by God and the American people.[11]

While the people retain their virtue and vigilance, no administration by any extreme of wickedness or folly can very seriously injure the government in the short space of four years.[12]

This . . . indicates an earnest desire on the part of the whole people, without regard to political differences, to save—not the country, because the country will save itself—but to save the institutions under which, in the last three-quarters of a century, we have grown to a great, an intelligent, and a happy people—the greatest, the most intelligent, and the happiest people in the world.[13]

But take men as a whole—I think he [Lincoln] thought better of them than they deserve. He had more faith in mankind, the masses, than any other man I ever knew.[14]

Isaac Arnold, longtime friend and early
biographer of Lincoln

*T*he trust which Abraham Lincoln had in himself and in the people was surprising and grand, but it was also enlightened and well founded. He knew the American people better than they knew themselves, and his trust was based upon this knowledge.[15]

Frederick Douglass, former slave and abolitionist

If the people remain right, your public men can never betray you. . . . Cultivate and protect that sentiment [that the principles of liberty are eternal] and your ambitious leaders will be reduced to the position of servants instead of masters.[16]

Allow me to say that you, as a portion of the great American people, need only to maintain your composure, stand up to your sober convictions of right, to your obligations to the Constitution, and act in accordance with those sober convictions, and the clouds now on the horizon will be dispelled, and we shall have a bright and glorious future.[17]

We are bound together in Christianity, civilization, and patriotism, and our attachment to our country and our whole country. While some of us may differ in political opinions, still we are all united in one feeling for the Union. We all believe in the maintenance of the Union, of every star and stripe of the glorious flag.[18]

The people know their rights, and they are never slow to assert and maintain them, when they are invaded.[19]

The most reliable indication of public purpose in this country is derived through our popular elections.[20]

The people of these United States are the rightful masters of both congresses and courts, not to overthrow the Constitution, but to overthrow the men who pervert the Constitution.[21]

Lincoln was the apostle of the common people. Their rights, their conditions, their hardships, their opportunities, their aspirations, their hopes, their joys and their sorrows—all these were subjects upon which his mind brooded and sought to work out plans for their betterment and happiness. No man ever knew the common people better than he, or was closer in sympathy with them. Having sprung from the innumerable common throng, his heart never ceased to beat in sympathy with them. Besides, he was endowed with that best sense—common sense. This, with his broad, clear grasp of every subject that touched the interest of the masses, made him preeminently the advocate of the rights of the common people.[22]

Judge Owen T. Reeves, soldier and legal scholar

It is not the qualified voters, but the qualified voters who choose to vote, that constitute the political power of the State.[23]

It is true . . . that very great responsibility rests upon me in the position to which the votes of the American people have called me. I am deeply sensible of that weighty responsibility. . . . I turn, then, and look to the American people, and to that God who has never forsaken them.[24]

If we have patience, if we restrain ourselves, if we allow ourselves not to run off in a passion, I still have confidence that the Almighty, the Maker of the universe, will, through the instrumentality of this great and intelligent people, bring us through this as he has through all the other difficulties of our country.[25]

The resources, advantages, and powers of the American people are very great, and they have, consequently succeeded to equally great responsibilities. It seems to have devolved upon them to test whether a government established on the principles of human freedom can be maintained against an effort to build one upon the exclusive foundation of human bondage.[26]

5

Kindness

THERE ARE MANY STORIES about Lincoln's kindness. As a youngster and as a young man, he was always rescuing friends or animals from calamity. As a lawyer, he many times offered to argue the case of some unfortunate person who could not afford counsel. Sometimes, when he thought he had been overpaid for legal work, he would return the money that he perceived to be in excess of what he was due.

But perhaps the supreme example of Lincoln's kindness was his willingness as president to work late hours, poring over the army's court-martial cases in which soldiers had been sentenced to be shot. He read each one diligently, looking for an excuse to pardon the man and spare his life. He continued to do this despite the protests of his generals, who claimed he was undermining discipline.

I am a patient man—always willing to forgive
on the Christian terms of repentance; and also to
give ample time for repentance.[1]

I shall do nothing in malice. What I deal with is
too vast for malicious dealing.[2]

I can only say that I have acted upon my best
convictions, without selfishness or malice, and
that by the help of God I shall continue to do so.[3]

Some of my generals complain that I impair discipline by my frequent pardons and reprieves;
but it rests me, after a day's hard work, that I can
find some excuse for saving some poor fellow's
life, and I shall go to bed happy tonight as I
think how joyous the signing of this name will
make himself, his family, and friends.[4]

I must say, and I am proud to say, that I never was treated by anyone with more kindness and cordiality than was shown me by the great and good man, Abraham Lincoln, by the grace of God president of the United States.[5]

> *Sojourner Truth, former slave and Underground Railroad "conductor" who visited Lincoln at the White House in October 1864*

Human nature will not change. In any future great national trial, compared with the men of this, we shall have as weak and as strong, as silly and as wise, as bad and as good. Let us therefore study the incidents of this, as philosophy to learn wisdom from, and none of them as wrongs to be revenged.[6]

I have an irrepressible desire to live till I can be assured that the world is a little better for my having lived in it.[7]

I am loath to close. We are not enemies but friends. We must not be enemies. Though passion may have strained, it must not break our bonds of affection. The mystic chords of memory, stretching from every battlefield and patriot grave to every living heart and hearthstone all over this broad land, will yet swell the chorus of the Union when again touched, as surely they will be, by the better angels of our nature.[8]

*H*e was one of the few great rulers whose wisdom increased with his power, and whose spirit grew gentler and tenderer as his triumphs were multiplied.[9]

> *James A. Garfield, a Union officer, politician,*
> *and the twentieth president of the United States*
> *(the second president to be assassinated in office)*

On the whole, my impression is that mercy bears richer fruits than any other attribute.[10]

*H*e would be just as kind and generous as his judgment would let him be—no more. If he ever deviated from this rule, it was to save life.[11]

Leonard Swett

In all our rejoicings, let us neither express nor cherish any hard feelings toward any citizen who, by his vote, has differed with us. Let us at all times remember that all American citizens are brothers of common country, and should do well together in the bonds of fraternal feeling.[12]

It is no pleasure to me to triumph over anyone.[13]

☆ ☆ ☆

If a man had more than one life, I think a little hanging would not hurt this one, but after he is once dead we cannot bring him back, no matter how sorry we may be, so the boy shall be pardoned.[14]

$\mathcal{N}$o man clothed with such vast power ever wielded it more tenderly and more forbearingly. No man holding in his hands the key of life and death ever pardoned so many offenders, and so easily.[15]

> *Schuyler Colfax, vice president in the first*
> *Ulysses S. Grant administration*

I am naturally antislavery. If slavery is not wrong, nothing is wrong. I cannot remember when I did not so think, and feel.[16]

I am most happy to meet you [soldiers] on this occasion. I understand that it has been your honorable privilege to stand, for a brief period, in the defense of your country, and that now you are on your way to your homes. I congratulate you, and those who are waiting to bid you welcome home from the war; and permit me, in the name of the people, to thank you for the part you have taken in this struggle for the life of the nation.[17]

6

Liberty

LINCOLN RECOGNIZED THAT LIBERTY meant different things to different Americans, and he fought hard to preserve the liberties he believed the Founding Fathers had intended. He did not agree with Stephen A. Douglas, who contended that the writers of the Declaration of Independence never intended for African Americans to be included when they said "all men" were "created equal." Lincoln believed that everyone, regardless of race, at least had the right to "eat the bread they earned."

Lincoln also believed that although the framers of the government originally allowed slavery, the Founding Fathers intended to ensure equally the pursuit of life, liberty, and happiness to all—regardless of race. This love of liberty, and his fear that the American people might one day lose it, motivated Lincoln more than anything else.

The fight must go on. The cause of civil liberty must not be surrendered at the end of one or even one hundred defeats.[1]

What is it that we hold most dear amongst us? Our own liberty and prosperity. What has ever threatened our liberty and prosperity, save and except this institution of slavery?[2]

Those who deny freedom to others deserve it not for themselves; and, under a just God, cannot long retain it.[3]

Our reliance is in the love of liberty which God has planted in our bosoms. Our defense is in the preservation of the spirit which prized liberty as the heritage of all men, in all lands, everywhere. Destroy this spirit and you have planted the seeds of despotism around your own doors. Familiarize yourselves with the chains of bondage, and you are preparing your own limbs to wear them.[4]

The world has never had a good definition of the word *liberty*, and the American people, just now, are much in want of one. We all declare for liberty; but in using the same word we do not all mean the same thing. With some the word *liberty* may mean for each man to do as he pleases with himself, and the product of his labor; while with others the same word may mean for some men to do as they please with other men, and the product of other men's labor. Here are two, not only different, but incompatible things, called by the same name, liberty.[5]

I believe the declaration that "all men are created equal" is the great fundamental principle upon which our free institutions rest.[6]

They were the pillars of the temple of liberty; and now, that they have crumbled away, that temple must fall, unless we, their descendants, supply their places with other pillars, hewn from the solid quarry of sober reason.[7]

There is something back of these, entwining itself more closely about the human heart. That
something is the principle of "Liberty to all"—
the principle that clears the path for all, gives
hope to all, and, by consequence, enterprise and
industry to all.[8]

*H*e was advised long before 1860, by some of
his more intimate friends, that his positions on
the subject of slavery and human rights would
be prejudicial to his party and to himself personally. He paid no attention to such admoni-
tions. The question with him was whether the
thing was right, and not what his friends may
have thought about the expediency of it.[9]

> *Judge Lawrence Weldon, legal associate*
> *of Lincoln*

I want every man to have a chance, and I believe
a black man is entitled to it—in which he can
better his condition.[10]

Let every American, every lover of liberty, every well-wisher to his posterity, swear by the blood of the Revolution never to violate in the least particular the laws of the country, and never to tolerate their violation by others.[11]

Our progress in degeneracy appears to me to be pretty rapid. As a nation we began by declaring that "all men are created equal." We now practically read it "all men are created equal, except Negroes." When the Know-Nothings [a nativist political party in the 1850s] get control, it will read "all men are created equal, except Negroes and foreigners and Catholics." When it comes to this, I shall prefer emigrating to some country where they make no pretense of loving liberty—to Russia, for instance, where despotism can be taken pure and without the base alloy of hypocrisy.[12]

*I*n all my interviews with Mr. Lincoln I was impressed with his entire freedom from popular prejudice against the colored race. He was the first great man that I talked with in the United States freely, who in no single instance reminded me of the difference between himself and myself, of the difference of color. . . . Then, too, there was another feeling that I had with reference to him, and that was that while I felt in his presence I was in the presence of a very great man, as great as the greatest, I felt as though I could go and put my hand on him if I wanted to, to put my hand on his shoulder. Of course I did not do it, but I felt that I could. I felt as though I was in the presence of a big brother, and that there was safety in his atmosphere.[13]

Frederick Douglass

*A*lthough volume upon volume is written to prove slavery a good thing, we never hear of the man who wishes to take the good of it, by being a slave himself.[14]

My friends, I have detained you about as long as I desired to do, and I have only to say, let us discard all this quibbling about this man and the other man—this race and that race and the other race being inferior, and therefore they must be placed in an inferior position. Let us discard all these things, and unite as one people throughout this land, until we shall once more stand up declaring that all men are created equal.[15]

That is the issue that will continue in this country when these poor tongues of Judge [Stephen A.] Douglas and myself shall be silent. It is the eternal struggle between these two principles—right and wrong—throughout the world. They are the two principles that have stood face to face from the beginning of time; and will ever continue to struggle. The one is the common right of humanity, and the other the divine right of kings. It is the same principle in whatever shape it develops itself. It is the same spirit that says, "You toil and work and earn bread, and I'll eat it."[16]

*B*ut the inevitable topic to which he returned with the most frequency, and to which
he clung with all the grasp of his soul, was the
practical character of the Declaration of Independence in announcing the Liberty and
Equality of all men.[17]

> *Charles Sumner, senator (R-MA) and*
> *friend of Lincoln*

Theirs [our American ancestors] was the task—
and nobly they performed it—to possess themselves, and through themselves us, of this goodly
land, and to uprear upon its hills and its valleys a
political edifice of liberty and equal rights; 'tis
ours only to transmit these—the former unpro-
faned by the foot of an invader, the latter unde-
cayed by the lapse of time and untorn by
usurpation—to the latest generation that fate
shall permit the world to know.[18]

*H*is great mission was to accomplish two things: first, to save his country from dismemberment and ruin; and second, to free his country from the great crime of slavery. To do one or the other, or both, he must have the earnest sympathy and the powerful cooperation of his loyal fellow-countrymen. Without this primary and essential condition to success his efforts must have been vain and utterly fruitless. Had he put the abolition of slavery before the salvation of the Union, he would have inevitably driven from him a powerful class of the American people and rendered resistance to rebellion impossible. Viewed from the genuine abolition ground, Mr. Lincoln seemed tardy, cold, dull, and indifferent; but measuring him by the sentiment of his country, a sentiment he was bound as a statesman to consult, he was swift, zealous, radical, and determined.[19]

Frederick Douglass

Common Sense

THOSE PEOPLE WHO KNEW Lincoln were always impressed with his abundant common sense. Lincoln himself claimed that although his mind worked very slowly, it was like steel—once something had been etched into it, it could not be removed. Lincoln was fond of repeating many of the anecdotes and jewels of wisdom he had accumulated over the years in speeches and letters he authored.

Some of the witticisms that are attributed to Lincoln today were probably common expressions of his time, but it is difficult to separate these from those that originated with him. Regardless of whether they were started by Lincoln or someone else, he used each of these gems to communicate a worthy point to the listener, and today they represent timeless wisdom worth remembering.

When I have friends who disagree with each other, I am very slow to take sides in their quarrel.[1]

When one is embarrassed, usually the shortest way to get through with it is to quit talking or thinking about it, and go at something else.[2]

Men are not flattered by being shown that there has been a difference of purpose between the Almighty and them.[3]

Common-looking people are the best in the world; that is the reason the Lord makes so many of them.[4]

I am never easy now, when I am handling a thought, till I have bounded it north and bounded it south, and bounded it east and bounded it west.[5]

*T*he characteristic that struck me most about [Lincoln] was his superabundance of common sense. His power of managing men, of deciding and avoiding difficult questions, surpassed that of any man I ever met. A keen insight of human nature had been cultivated by the trials and struggles of his early life. He knew the people and how to reach them better than any man of his time.[6]

> *Chauncey M. Depew, state representative from*
> *New York and orator*

*H*alf-finished work generally proves to be labor lost.[7]

*T*he better part of one's life consists of his friendships.[8]

*T*he loss of enemies does not compensate for the loss of friends.[9]

Quarrel not at all. No man resolved to make the most of himself can spare time for personal contention. Still less can he afford to take all the consequences, including the vitiating of his temper and the loss of self-control. Yield larger things to which you can show no more than equal right; and yield lesser ones, though clearly your own. Better give your path to a dog than be bitten by him in contesting for the right. Even killing the dog would not cure the bite.[10]

A man has no time to spend half his life in quarrels.[11]

Common people . . . are more easily influenced and informed through the medium of a broad illustration than in any other way.[12]

Persuade your neighbor to compromise whenever you can.[13]

If you would win a man to your cause, first convince him that you are his sincere friend. Therein is a drop of honey that catches his heart, which . . . when once gained, you will find but little trouble in convincing his judgment of the justice of your cause.[14]

Bad promises are better broken than kept.[15]

[Lincoln] was a master of statement. Few have equaled him in the ability to strip a truth of surplus verbiage and present it in its naked strength.[16]

William Jennings Bryan, politician and orator
of the late nineteenth century

All creation is a mine, and every man, a miner.[17]

If you make a bad bargain, hug it all the tighter.[18]

Nothing valuable can be lost by taking time. If there be an object to hurry any of you, in hot haste, to a step which you would never take deliberately, that object will be frustrated by taking time; but no good object can be frustrated by it.[19]

Even those who only knew him through his public utterances obtained a tolerably clear idea of his character and his personality. The image of the man went through his words, and those who read them, knew him.[20]

Frederick Douglass

What is to be will be, and no cares of ours can arrest nor reverse the decree.[21]

As a general rule, I abstain from reading the reports of attacks upon myself, wishing not to be provoked by that which I cannot properly offer an answer.[22]

8

Character

Dictionaries tell us that character is the moral or ethical structure of a person. With the possible exception of George Washington, Lincoln is admired for his character more than any other American leader. Honesty, honor, wisdom, vision, kindness—all of these qualities are attributed to Lincoln.

Even so, Lincoln was not universally admired in his lifetime. In fact, many hated him. However, by the time he had begun his second term as president, he had cultivated the respect of friends and enemies alike. Both friend and foe recognized that he had fought his way up from poverty and ignorance. Many saw him as a patient, benevolent leader who brought the nation through its most difficult hour. Most realized that he endured a great deal of hostility on the part of his fellow man and rarely returned anything but kindness.

A man's character is like a tree and his reputation like its shadow; the shadow is what we
think of it; the tree is the real thing.[1]

I [wish to be] so clear that no honest man can
misunderstand me and no dishonest one successfully misrepresent me.[2]

I have not permitted myself, gentlemen, to con-
clude that I am the best man in the country; but
I am reminded, in this connection, of a story of
an old Dutch farmer, who remarked to a com-
panion once that "It was not best to swap horses
when crossing streams."[3]

I have endured a great deal of ridicule without
much malice; and have received a great deal of
kindness, not quite free from ridicule. I am used
to it.[4]

The world shall know that I will keep my faith to friends and enemies, come what will.[5]

I want in all cases to do right, and most particularly so in all cases with women.[6]

The beauty of his character was its entire simplicity. . . . True to nature, true to himself, he was true to everybody and everything about and around him. When he was ignorant on any subject, no matter how simple it might make him appear he was always willing to acknowledge it. His whole aim in life was to be true to himself and being true to himself he could be false to no one.[7]

Joshua Speed, one of Lincoln's closest friends

Many free countries have lost their liberty; and ours may lose hers; but if she shall, be it my proudest plume, not that I was the last to desert, but that I never deserted her.[8]

Most certainly I intend no injustice to any, and if I have done any I deeply regret it.[9]

To me he always seemed to be a very great man. In all the qualities of true greatness of character and mind he was the equal, if not the superior, of all the great statesmen I have ever known. Of all these public men, none seemed to have so little pride of opinion. He was always learning and did not adhere to views which he found to be erroneous, simply because he had once formed and held them.[10]

John B. Alley

I have never done an official act with a view to promote my personal aggrandizement, and I don't like to begin now.[11]

At every step we must be true to the main purpose.[12]

$\mathcal{A}$s a political leader he was actuated in his movements by strong convictions of duty, and had great power in convincing people of the righteousness of his cause. No man could stand in his presence and hear him without feeling sure of the honesty of his purposes and declarations, or of the strength of his arguments in behalf of whatever cause he championed.[13]

> *Shelby Cullom, senator (R-IL) and friend of Lincoln*

I am very little inclined on any occasion to say anything unless I hope to produce some good by it.[14]

I am very sure that if I do not go away from here a wiser man, I shall go away a better man, for having learned here what a very poor sort of a man I am.[15]

Whatever woman may cast her lot with mine, should any ever do so, it is my intention to do all in my power to make her happy and contented; and there is nothing I can imagine that would make me more unhappy than to fail in the effort.[16]

I do not consider that I have ever accomplished anything without God; and if it is His will that I must die by the hand of an assassin, I must be resigned. I must do my duty as I see it, and leave the rest with God.[17]

Important principles may and must be inflexible.[18]

No men living are more worthy to be trusted than those who toil up from poverty—none less inclined to take, or touch, aught which they have not honestly earned.[19]

Lincoln . . . has taught us, that no party or partisan can escape responsibility to the people; that no party advantage, or presumed party advantage, should ever swerve us from the plain path of duty, which is ever the path of honor and distinction. He emphasized his words by his daily life and deeds. He showed to the world by his lofty example, as well as by precept and maxim, that there are times when the voice of partisanship should be hushed and that of patriotism only be heeded.[20]

> *William McKinley, a Union officer, Ohio*
> *politician, and the twenty-fifth president of the*
> *United States (the third president to be*
> *assassinated while in office)*

Democracy

LINCOLN'S CONCEPT OF DEMOCRACY is rooted in the Declaration of Independence—which he paraphrased as: "No man is good enough to govern another man without that other's consent." He also believed that elected representatives are bound to carry out the known wishes of their constituents. He called this the "great living principle" of democracy.

Although he recognized that, in allowing slavery, the Constitution had compromised the ideals expressed in the Declaration, he believed that this was an error that would be inevitably corrected. Consequently, he considered American democratic government, although imperfect, to be the best form of government known to man. He feared that if his generation did not preserve the Union, democracy would be forever lost and fail to benefit future generations.

Our government rests in public opinion. Who-
ever can change public opinion can change the
government.[1]

I have never had a feeling, politically, that did
not spring from the sentiments embodied in the
Declaration of Independence.[2]

I go for all sharing the privileges of the government who assist in bearing its burdens.[3]

I am exceedingly anxious that this Union, the
Constitution, and the liberties of the people shall
be perpetuated in accordance with the original
idea for which that struggle was made, and I shall
be most happy indeed if I shall be an humble instrument in the hands of the Almighty, and of
this, his almost chosen people, for perpetuating
the object of that great struggle.[4]

Most governments have been based, practically, on the denial of the equal rights of men. . . . Ours began by affirming those rights.[5]

The legitimate object of government is to do for a community of people whatever they need to have done, but cannot do at all, or cannot so well do, for themselves, in their separate and individual capacities. In all that the people can individually do as well for themselves, government ought not to interfere.[6]

Lincoln believed in the uplifting of influences of free government, and that by giving all a chance we could get higher average results for the people than where governments are exclusive and opportunities are limited to the few. No American ever did so much as he to enlarge these opportunities.[7]

William McKinley

In this and like communities, public sentiment is everything. With public sentiment, nothing can fail; without it, nothing can succeed. Consequently he who molds public sentiment goes deeper than he who enacts statutes or pronounces decisions. He makes statutes and decisions possible or impossible to be executed.[8]

I trust I understand, and truly estimate, the right of self-government. My faith in the proposition that each man should do precisely as he pleases with all which is exclusively his own, lies at the foundation of the sense of justice there is in me.[9]

I consider the central idea pervading this struggle is the necessity that is upon us, of proving that popular government is not an absurdity. We must settle this question now, whether in a free government the minority have the right to break up the government whenever they choose.[10]

As I would not be a slave, so I would not be a master. This expresses my idea of democracy. Whatever differs from this, to the extent of the difference, is no democracy.[11]

He did not hesitate, he did not doubt, he did not falter; but at once resolved that at whatever peril, at whatever cost, the union of the States would be preserved. A patriot himself, his faith was strong and unwavering in the patriotism of his countrymen. . . . But in the midst of all this tumult and timidity, and against all this, Abraham Lincoln was clear in his duty, and had an oath in heaven. He calmly and bravely heard the voice of doubt and fear all around him; but he had an oath in heaven, and there was not power enough on the earth to make this honest boatman, backwoodsman, and broad-handed splitter of rails evade or violate that sacred oath.[12]

Frederick Douglass

And this issue embraces more than the fate of these United States. It presents to the whole family of man the question whether a constitutional republic or democracy—a government of the people, by the same people—can or cannot maintain its territorial integrity against its own domestic foes. It presents the question whether discontented individuals, too few in numbers to control administration according to organic law, in any case, can always, upon the pretenses made in this case, or on any other pretenses, or arbitrarily without any pretense, break up their government and thus practically put an end to free government upon the earth. It forces us to ask: "Is there, in all republics, this inherent and fatal weakness?" "Must a government, of necessity, be too strong for the liberties of its own people, or too weak to maintain its own existence?"[13]

Let every man remember that to violate the law is to trample on the blood of his father, and to tear the charter of his own and his children's liberty.[14]

A free people, in times of peace and quiet—
when pressed by no common danger—naturally
divide into parties. At such times, the man who
is of neither party, is not—cannot be—of any
consequence.[15]

The true rule in determining to embrace or re-
ject anything, is not whether it have any evil in it,
but whether it have more of evil than of good.
There are few things wholly evil or wholly good.
Almost everything, especially of government policy, is an inseparable compound of the two; so
that our best judgment of the preponderance between them is continually demanded.[16]

To give the victory to the right, not bloody bul-
lets, but peaceful ballots only, are necessary.
Thanks to our good old constitution, and organ-
ization under it, these alone are necessary. It only
needs that every right thinking man shall go to
the polls and, without fear or prejudice, vote as
he thinks.[17]

Finally, I insist, that if there is anything which it is the duty of the whole people to never entrust to any hands but their own, that thing is the preservation and perpetuity of their own liberties, and institutions.[18]

If the politicians and leaders of parties were as true as the people, there would be little fear that the peace of the country would be disturbed. I have been selected to fill an important office for a brief period, and am now, in your eyes, invested with an influence which will soon pass away; but should my administration prove to be a very wicked one, or what is more probable, a very foolish one, if you, the people, are but true to yourselves and to the Constitution, there is but little harm I can do, thank God![19]

Liberty to all"—the principle that clears the path for all—gives hope to all—and, by consequence, enterprise, and industry to all.[20]

A house divided against itself cannot stand. I believe this government cannot endure permanently half slave and half free. I do not expect the Union to be dissolved—I do not expect the house to fall—but I do expect it will cease to be divided. It will become all one thing, or all the other. Either the opponents of slavery will arrest the further spread of it, and place it where the public mind shall rest in the belief that it is in the course of ultimate extinction; or its advocates will push it forward till it shall become alike lawful in all the States, old as well as new, North as well as South.[21]

10

Perseverance

ONE OF LINCOLN'S GREATEST strengths as a leader was his ability to identify the most important problem and concentrate every resource on solving it. He admitted that he was sometimes slow making up his mind as to what to do, but once he did, he never wavered regarding his purpose.

As president, Lincoln sought to "learn God's will" on important issues, and once he believed he'd determined that will, he never hesitated in following it. His commitment to maintenance of the Union is a prime example. He was willing to do anything, even ignore portions of the Constitution, to maintain the sovereignty of the United States of America. He considered this equivalent to "sacrificing a limb" in order to "save a life."

Always bear in mind that your own resolution to succeed is more important than any other one thing.[1]

Must is the word. I know not how to aid you, save in the assurance of one of mature age, and much severe experience, that you cannot fail, if you resolutely determine that you will not.[2]

The probability that we may fall in the struggle ought not to deter us from the support of a cause we believe to be just.[3]

By all means, don't say "if I can"; say "I will."[4]

I expect to maintain this contest until successful, or till I die, or am conquered, or my term expires, or Congress or the country forsakes me.[5]

Lincoln describing his prosecution of the war

*W*hilst other boys were idling away their time, Lincoln was at home studying hard.[6]

> *Nat Grigsby, childhood friend of Lincoln and a Union soldier*

*T*he way for a young man to rise, is to improve himself every way he can, never suspecting that anybody wishes to hinder him. Allow me to assure you, that suspicion and jealousy never did help any man in any situation. There may sometimes be ungenerous attempts to keep a young man down; and they will succeed, too, if he allows his mind to be diverted from its true channel to brood over the attempted injury.[7]

*U*pon the subject of education, not presuming to dictate any plan or system respecting it, I can only say that I view it as the most important subject which we as a people can be engaged in.[8]

*I*n his rise from the most abject poverty and ignorance to a position of high usefulness and power, he taught the world one of the greatest of all lessons. In fighting his own battle up from obscurity and squalor, he fought the battle of every other individual and race that is down, and so helped to pull up every other human who was down. People so often forget that by every inch that the lowest man crawls up he makes it easier for every other man to get up. Today, throughout the world, because Lincoln lived, struggled, and triumphed, every boy who is ignorant, is in poverty, is despised or discouraged, holds his head a little higher. His heart beats a little faster, his ambition to do something and be something is a little stronger, because Lincoln blazed the way.[9]

> *Booker T. Washington, former slave*
> *and educator*

I am always for the man who wishes to work.[10]

The leading rule for the lawyer, as for the man of every other calling, is diligence. Leave nothing for tomorrow which can be done today.[11]

Universal idleness would speedily result in universal ruin.[12]

The result is not doubtful. We shall not fail—if we stand firm, we shall not fail.[13]

Determine that the thing can and shall be done, and then we shall find the way.[14]

Adhere to your purpose and you will soon feel as well as you ever did. On the contrary, if you falter, and give up, you will lose the power to keep any resolution, and will regret it all your life. Take the advice of a friend . . . and stick to your purpose.[15]

*I*n the log schoolhouse, which he could visit but little, he was taught only reading, writing, and elementary arithmetic. Among the people of the settlement, bush farmers, and small tradesmen, he found none of uncommon intelligence or education; but some of them had a few books, which he borrowed eagerly. . . . Every printed page that fell into his hands he would greedily devour, and his family and friends watched him with wonder, as an uncouth boy, after his daily work, crouched in a corner of the log cabin or outside under a tree, absorbed in a book while munching his supper of corn bread.[16]

Carl Shurtz, editor, soldier, and politician

I'll study and get ready, and then the chance will come.[17]

*W*ork, work, work, is the main thing.[18]

*H*e was always calculating, always planning ahead. His ambition was a little engine that knew no rest.[19]

William Herndon

If you intend to go to work, there is no better place than right where you are.[20]

I am a living witness that any one of your children may look to come here [to the White House] as my father's child has.[21]

*M*r. Lincoln . . . was a terribly firm man when he set his foot down—none of us—no man nor woman could rule him after he had made up his mind.[22]

Mary Todd Lincoln

As a pilot I have used my best exertions to keep afloat our Ship of State, and shall be glad to resign my trust at the appointed time to another pilot more skillful and successful than I may prove. In every case and at all hazards the government must be perpetuated. Relying, as I do, upon the Almighty Power, and encouraged as I am by these resolutions which you have just read, with the support which I receive from Christian men, I shall not hesitate to use all the means at my control to secure the termination of this rebellion, and will hope for success.[23]

Humor

ALTHOUGH LINCOLN'S LEADERSHIP AND generous heart are world renowned, many people are unaware of his tremendous wit and love of humor. Lincoln said that he cared nothing for the common vices of his day, such as drinking or gambling, but he loved to tell jokes and funny stories. He considered a witty story a sort of "tonic" or medicine.

Lincoln's storytelling skills were instrumental in his political success. Senator Stephen A. Douglas, a frequent object of Lincoln's funny stories, said that every one of them "seems like a whack across my back." By the time Lincoln was president, he was telling and reading humorous stories as much for his own benefit as anyone else's. He used humor to help relieve the stress and personal losses he endured while in the White House.

Laughter [is] the joyous, beautiful, universal evergreen of life.[1]

It was a common notion that those who laughed heartily often never amounted to much—never made great men. If this be the case, farewell to all my glory.[2]

I have heard some things from New York; and if they are true, one might well say of your party there, as a drunken fellow once said when he heard the reading of an indictment for hog-stealing. The clerk read on till he got to and through the words, "did steal, take, and carry away ten boars, ten sows, ten shoats, and ten pigs," at which he exclaimed, "Well, by golly, that is the most equally divided gang of hogs I ever did hear of!" If there is any other gang of hogs more equally divided than the Democrats of New York are about this time, I have not heard of it.[3]

I have now come to the conclusion never again to think of marrying, and for this reason—I can never be satisfied with anyone who would be blockhead enough to have me.[4]

I feel like I once did when I met a woman riding horseback in the woods. As I stopped to let her pass, she also stopped, and, looking at me intently, said: "I do believe you are the ugliest man I ever saw." Said I, "Madam, you are probably right, but I can't help it!" "No," said she, "you can't help it, but you might stay at home!"[5]

Mr. Chairman, this work is exclusively the work of politicians; a set of men who have interests aside from the interests of the people, and who, to say the most of them, are, taken as a mass, at least one long step removed from honest men. I say this with the greater freedom because, being a politician myself, none can regard it as personal.[6]

*E*very one of his stories seems like a whack across my back. . . . Nothing else—not any of his arguments or any of his replies to my questions—disturbs me. But when he begins to tell a story, I feel that I am to be overmatched.[7]

Stephen A. Douglas

I remember being once much amused at seeing two partially intoxicated men engaged in a fight with their great coats on, which fight, after a long and rather harmless contest, ended in each having fought himself out of his own coat and into that of the other.[8]

describing how two political parties had
swapped positions on an issue

I was not very much accustomed to flattery, and it came the sweeter to me. I was rather like the Hoosier with the gingerbread, when he said he reckoned he loved it better than any other man, and got less of it.[9]

Others have been made fools of by the girls, but this can never with truth be said of me. I most emphatically, in this instance, made a fool of myself.[10]

We have all heard of the animal standing in doubt between two stacks of hay and starving to death. The like of that would never happen to General [Lewis] Cass. Place the stacks a thousand miles apart, he would stand stock-still midway between them, and eat them both at once, and the green grass along the line would be apt to suffer some, too.[11]

ridiculing Lewis Cass, the Democrats'
presidential candidate in 1848

Please have the Adjutant General ascertain whether 2nd Lieut. of Co. D. 2nd Infantry— Alexander E. Drake—is not entitled to promotion. His wife thinks he is.[12]

Has it not got down as thin as the homeopathic soup that was made by boiling the shadow of a pigeon that had starved to death?[13]

> *a description of how "thin" was one of Stephen*
> *A. Douglas's political arguments*

Dear Sir: Says Tom to John, "Here's your old rotten wheelbarrow. I've broke it, usin' on it. I wish you would mend it, 'case I shall want to borrow it this arter-noon."[14]

> *Lincoln telling a joke while asking for a new*
> *railroad pass*

Sending men [to Gen. George B. McClellan] is like shoveling fleas across a barnyard—half of them never get there.[15]

> *expressing frustration over McClellan's*
> *constant demand for reinforcements during*
> *the Peninsula campaign*

*H*is expression in repose was sad and dull; but
his ever-recurring humor, at short intervals,
flashed forth with the brilliancy of an electric
light. I observed but two well-defined expressions
in his countenance; one, that of a pure, thought-
ful, honest man, absorbed by a sense of duty and
responsibility; the other, that of a humorist so
full of fun that he could not keep it all in. His
power of analysis was wonderful. He strengthened every case he stated, and no anecdote or
joke ever lost force or effect from his telling. He
invariably carried the listener with him to the
very climax, and when that was reached in relat-
ing a humorous story, he laughed all over. His
large mouth assumed an unexpected and comical
shape, the skin on his nose gathered into wrin-
kles, and his small eyes, though partly closed,
emitted infectious rays of fun. It was not only the
aptness of his stories, but his way of telling them,
and his own unfeigned enjoyment, that gave
them zest, even among the gravest men and
upon the most serious occasions.[16]

James B. Fry, U.S. provost marshal general

The opinion of Mr. Jefferson, in one branch at least, is, in the hands of Mr. Polk, like McFingal's gun—"bears wide and kicks the owner over."[17]

This he [Stephen A. Douglas] cannot deny; and so he remembers to forget it.[18]

A man in Cortlandt county raised a porker of such unusual size that strangers went out of their way to see it. One of them the other day met the old gentleman and inquired about the animal. "Wall, yes," the old fellow said; "he'd got such a critter, mighty big un; but he guessed he would have to charge him about a shillin' for lookin' at him." The stranger looked at the old man for a minute or so; pulled out the desired coin, handed it to him and started to go off. "Hold on," said the other, "don't you want to see the hog?" "No," said the stranger, "I have seen as big a hog as I want to see!"[19]

12

Hope

LINCOLN HELD THAT AMERICA offered mankind
the greatest hope for the future. He believed several factors contributed to this great hope. The
American people, he believed, were so resourceful
that they were unconquerable by anyone but
themselves. America's natural resources were so
vast that they represented the "choicest bounties
of heaven." American government, in proposing
equal opportunity for all, was the best yet formed
by man. Finally, he believed that God would forever bless America if her people would continue
to seek his will and do what is "right."

It was because of his great confidence in what
America could do for mankind that he considered it essential he and his generation make whatever sacrifices were necessary in order to preserve
the "last, best hope of earth."

Let us readopt the Declaration of Independence, and with it the practices and policy which harmonize with it. Let North and South—let all Americans—let all lovers of liberty everywhere join in the great and good work. If we do this, we shall not only have saved the Union, but we shall have so saved it as to make and to keep it forever worthy of the saving. We shall have so saved it that the succeeding millions of free happy people, the world over, shall rise up and call us blessed to the latest generations.[1]

Let us be quite sober. Let us diligently apply the means, never doubting that a just God, in his own good time, will give us the rightful result.[2]

Yet, under all circumstances, trusting to our Maker, and through his wisdom and beneficence, to the great body of our people, we will not despair, or despond.[3]

But this government must be preserved in spite of the acts of any man or set of men. It is worthy of your every effort. Nowhere in the world is presented a government of so much liberty and equality. To the humblest and poorest amongst us are held out the highest privileges and positions. The present moment finds me at the White House, yet there is as good a chance for your children as there was for my father's.[4]

It is difficult to make a man miserable when he feels worthy of himself and claims kindred to the great God who made him.[5]

With malice toward none; with charity for all; with firmness in the right, as God gives us to see the right, let us strive on to finish the work we are in; to bind up the nation's wounds; to care for him who shall have borne the battle, and for his widow, and his orphan—to do all which may achieve and cherish a just and a lasting peace among ourselves, and with all nations.[6]

Fellow-citizens, we cannot escape history. We of this Congress and this administration will be remembered in spite of ourselves. No personal significance or insignificance can spare one or another of us. The fiery trial through which we pass will light us down, in honor or dishonor, to the latest generation. We say we are for the Union. The world will not forget that we say this. We know how to save the Union. The world knows we do know how to save it. We—even we here—hold the power and bear the responsibility. In giving freedom to the slave, we assure freedom to the free—honorable alike in what we give and what we preserve. We shall nobly save or meanly lose the last, best hope of earth. Other means may succeed; this could not fail. The way is plain, peaceful, generous, just—a way which, if followed, the world will forever applaud, and God must forever bless.[7]

The struggle of today is not altogether for today—it is for a vast future also.[8]

The power of hope upon the human exertion and happiness is wonderful.[9]

He saw clearly that the same high qualities, the same courage, and willingness for self-sacrifice, and devotion to the right as it was given them to see the right, belonged both to the men of the North and to the men of the South. As the years roll by, and as all of us, wherever we dwell, grow to feel an equal pride in the valor and self-devotion, alike of the men who wore the blue and the men who wore the gray, so this whole nation will grow to feel a peculiar sense of pride in the man whose blood was shed for the union of his people and for the freedom of a race; the lover of his country and all mankind; the mightiest of the mighty men who mastered the mighty days: Abraham Lincoln.[10]

Theodore Roosevelt, twenty-sixth president of the United States

$\mathcal{B}$y the same token that Lincoln made America free, he pushed back the boundaries of freedom everywhere, gave the spirit of liberty a wider influence throughout the world, and reestablished the dignity of man as man.[11]

Booker T. Washington

★ ★ ★

We thereby restore the national faith, the national confidence, the national feeling of brotherhood. We thereby reinstate the spirit of concession and compromise—that spirit which has never failed us in past perils, and which may be safely trusted for all the future.[12]

We are a great empire. We are eighty years old. We stand at once the wonder and admiration of the whole world, and we must inquire what it is that has given us so much prosperity, and we shall understand that to give up that one thing would be to give up all future prosperity. This cause is that every man can make himself. It has been said that such a race of prosperity has been run nowhere else.[13]

I wish you a long life and prosperity individually, and pray that with the perpetuity of those
institutions under which we have all so long lived
and prospered, our happiness may be secured,
our future made brilliant, and the glorious des-
tiny of our country established forever.[14]

We proposed to give all a chance; and we expect the weak to grow stronger, the ignorant,
wiser, and all better, and happier together.[15]

I have often inquired of myself, what great principle or idea it was that kept this Confederacy so
long together. It was not the mere matter of the
separation of the colonies from the mother land;
but something in that Declaration giving liberty,
not alone to the people of this country, but hope
to the world for all future time. It was that which
gave promise that in due time the weights should
be lifted from the shoulders of all men, and that
all should have an equal chance.[16]

The Gettysburg Address

FOURSCORE AND SEVEN YEARS ago our fathers brought forth on this continent a new nation, conceived in liberty, and dedicated to the proposition that all men are created equal.

Now we are engaged in a great civil war, testing whether that nation, or any nation so conceived and so dedicated, can long endure. We are met on a great battlefield of that war. We have come to dedicate a portion of that field as a final resting place for those who here gave their lives that that nation might live. It is altogether fitting and proper that we should do this.

But, in a larger sense, we cannot dedicate—we cannot consecrate—we cannot hallow—this ground. The brave men, living and dead, who struggled here, have consecrated it far above our poor power to add or detract. The world will little note nor long remember what we say here, but it can never forget what they did here. It is for us, the living, rather, to be dedicated here to

the unfinished work which they who fought here
have thus far so nobly advanced. It is rather for
us to be here dedicated to the great task remain-
ing before us—that from these honored dead we
take increased devotion to that cause for which
they gave the last full measure of devotion; that
we here highly resolve that these dead shall not
have died in vain; that this nation, under God,
shall have a new birth of freedom; and that
government of the people, by the people, for the
people, shall not perish from the earth.[1]

Excerpt from Lincoln's First Inaugural Address

I HOLD, THAT IN contemplation of universal law, and of the Constitution, the Union of these States is perpetual. Perpetuity is implied, if not expressed, in the fundamental law of all national governments. It is safe to assert that no government proper ever had a provision in its organic law for its own termination.

Continue to execute all the express provisions of our National Constitution, and the Union will endure forever—it being impossible to destroy it, except by some action not provided for in the instrument itself.

Again, if the United States be not a government proper, but an association of States in the nature of contract merely, can it, as a contract, be peaceably unmade by less than all the parties who made it? One party to a contract may violate it—

break it, so to speak; but does it not require all to lawfully rescind it?

Descending from these general principles, we find the proposition that, in legal contemplation, the Union is perpetual, confirmed by the history of the Union itself. The Union is much older than the Constitution. It was formed, in fact, by the Articles of Association in 1774. It was matured and continued by the Declaration of Independence in 1776. It was further matured and the faith of all the then thirteen States expressly plighted and engaged that it should be perpetual, by the Articles of Confederation in 1778. And finally, in 1787, one of the declared objects for ordaining and establishing the Constitution, was "to form a more perfect union."

But if destruction of the Union, by one, or by a part only, of the States, be lawfully possible, the Union is less perfect than before the Constitution, having lost the vital element of perpetuity.

It follows from these views that no State, upon its own mere motion, can lawfully get out of the Union, that resolves and ordinances to that effect are legally void; and that acts of violence, within any State or States, against the authority of the

United States, are insurrectionary or revolutionary, according to circumstances.

I therefore consider that, in view of the Constitution and the laws, the Union is unbroken; and, to the extent of my ability, I shall take care, as the Constitution itself expressly enjoins upon me, that the laws of the Union be faithfully executed in all the States. Doing this I deem to be only a simple duty on my part; and I shall perform it, so far as practicable, unless my rightful masters, the American people, shall withhold the

requisite means, or, in some authoritative manner, direct the contrary. I trust this will not be re-
garded as a menace, but only as the declared
purpose of the Union that it will constitutionally
defend, and maintain itself.[1]

Lincoln's Second Inaugural Address

AT THIS SECOND APPEARING to take the oath of the presidential office, there is less occasion for an extended address than there was at the first. Then a statement, somewhat in detail, of a course to be pursued, seemed fitting and proper. Now, at the expiration of four years, during which public declarations have been constantly called forth on every point and phase of the great contest which still absorbs the attention and engrosses the energies of the nation, little that is new could be presented. The progress of our arms, upon which all else chiefly depends, is as well known to the public as to myself; and it is, I trust, reasonably satisfactory and encouraging to all. With high hope for the future, no prediction in regard to it is ventured.

On the occasion corresponding to this four years ago, all thoughts were anxiously directed to an impending civil-war. All dreaded it—all sought

to avert it. While the inaugural address was being delivered from this place, devoted altogether to saving the Union without war, insurgent agents were in the city seeking to destroy it without war—seeking to dissolve the Union, and divide effects, by negotiation. Both parties deprecated war; but one of them would make war rather than let the nation survive; and the other would accept war rather than let it perish. And the war came.

One eighth of the whole population were colored slaves, not distributed generally over the Union, but localized in the Southern part of it. These slaves constituted a peculiar and powerful interest. All knew that this interest was, somehow, the cause of the war. To strengthen, perpetuate, and extend this interest was the object for which the insurgents would rend the Union, even by war; while the government claimed no right to do more than to restrict the territorial enlargement of it. Neither party expected for the war, the magnitude, or the duration, which it has already attained. Neither anticipated that the cause of the conflict might cease with, or even before, the conflict itself should cease. Each looked for an easier triumph, and a result less fundamental and astounding. Both read the same Bible, and pray to the same God; and each invokes his aid against the other. It may seem strange that any men should dare to ask a just God's assistance in wringing their bread from the sweat of other men's faces; but let us judge not that we be not judged. The prayers of both could not be answered; that of neither has been answered fully. The Almighty has his own purposes. "Woe unto the world because of offences! for it must needs be that offences come; but woe to that man by whom the offence cometh!" If we shall suppose that American Slavery is one of those offences which, in the providence of God, must needs come, but which, having continued through his appointed time, he now wills to remove, and that he gives to both North and South, this terrible war, as the woe due to those by whom the offence came, shall we discern therein any departure from those divine attributes which the believers in a Living God always ascribe to him? Fondly do we hope—fervently do we pray—that this mighty scourge of war may speedily pass away. Yet, if God wills that it continue, until all the wealth piled by the bondman's two hundred and fifty years of unrequited toil shall be sunk, and until every drop of blood drawn with the lash, shall be paid by another drawn with the sword, as was said three thousand years ago, so still it must be said "the judgments of the Lord, are true and righteous altogether."

With malice toward none; with charity for all; with firmness in the right, as God gives us to see the right, let us strive on to finish the work we are in; to bind up the nation's wounds; to care for him who shall have borne the battle, and for his widow, and his orphan—to do all which may achieve and cherish a just and a lasting peace among ourselves, and with all nations.[1]

First Annual Thanksgiving Day Proclamation

THE YEAR THAT IS drawing towards its close has been filled with the blessings of fruitful fields and healthful skies. To these bounties, which are so constantly enjoyed that we are prone to forget the source from which they come, others have been added, which are of so extraordinary a nature that they cannot fail to penetrate and soften the heart which is habitually insensible to the ever watchful providence of Almighty God.

In the midst of a civil war of unequaled magnitude and severity, which has sometimes seemed to foreign states to invite and to provoke their aggression, peace has been preserved with all nations, order has been maintained, the laws have been respected and obeyed, and harmony has prevailed everywhere, except in the theater of military conflict; while that theater has been greatly contracted by the advancing armies and navies of the Union.

Needful diversions of wealth and strength from the fields of peaceful industry to the national defence, have not arrested the plow, the shuttle, or the ship; the axe has enlarged the borders of our settlements, and the mines, as well of iron and coal as of the precious metals, have yielded even more abundantly than heretofore. Population has steadily increased, notwithstanding the waste that has been made in the camp, the siege and the battlefield, and the country, rejoicing in the consciousness of augmented strength and vigor, is permitted to expect continuance of years with large increase of freedom.

No human counsel hath devised nor hath any mortal hand worked out these great things. They are the gracious gifts of the Most High God, who, while dealing with us in anger for our sins, hath nevertheless remembered mercy.

It has seemed to me fit and proper that they should be solemnly, reverently, and gratefully acknowledged as with one heart and one voice by the whole American people. I do, therefore, invite my fellow-citizens in every part of the United States, and also those who are at sea and those who are sojourning in foreign lands, to set apart

and observe the last Thursday of November next as a day of thanksgiving and praise to our beneficent Father who dwelleth in the heavens. And I recommend to them that, while offering up the ascriptions justly due to him for such singular deliverances and blessings, they do also, with humble penitence for our national perverseness and disobedience, commend to his tender care all those who have become widows, orphans, mourners or sufferers in the lamentable civil strife in which we are unavoidably engaged, and fervently implore the interposition of the almighty hand to heal the wounds of the nation, and to restore it, as soon as may be consistent with the Divine purposes, to the full enjoyment of peace, harmony, tranquility and Union.[1]

Excerpt from Lincoln's First Address to Congress

THE CONSTITUTION PROVIDES, AND all the States have accepted the provision, that "the United States shall guarantee to every State in this Union a republican form of government." But if a State may lawfully go out of the Union, having done so, it may also discard the republican form of government; so that to prevent its going out is an indispensable means to the end of maintaining the guarantee mentioned; and when an end is lawful and obligatory, the indispensable means to it are also lawful and obligatory.

It was with the deepest regret that the executive found the duty of employing the war power in defense of the government forced upon him. He could but perform this duty or surrender the existence of the government. No compromise by public servants could, in this case, be a cure; not that compromises are not often proper, but that no popular government can long survive a marked precedent that those who carry an election can only save the government from immediate destruction by giving up the main point upon which the people gave the election. The people themselves, and not their servants, can safely reverse their own deliberate decisions.

As a private citizen the executive could not have consented that these institutions shall perish; much less could he, in betrayal of so vast and so sacred a trust as the free people have confided to him. He felt that he had no moral right to shrink, nor even to count the chances of his own life in what might follow. In full view of his great responsibility he has, so far, done what he has deemed his duty. You will now, according to your own judgment, perform yours.

He sincerely hopes that your views and your actions may so accord with his, as to assure all faithful citizens who have been disturbed in their rights of a certain and speedy restoration to them, under the Constitution and the laws.

And having thus chosen our course, without guile and with pure purpose, let us renew our trust in God, and go forward without fear and with manly hearts.[1]

Excerpt from the
Emancipation Proclamation

ON THE FIRST DAY of January, in the year of our Lord one thousand eight hundred and sixty-three, all persons held as slaves within any State or designated part of a State the people whereof shall then be in rebellion against the United States, shall be then, thenceforward, and forever free; and the Executive Government of the United States, including the military and naval authority thereof, will recognize and maintain the freedom of such persons, and will do no act or acts to repress such persons, or any of them, in any efforts they may make for their actual freedom. . . .

That all slaves of persons who shall hereafter be engaged in rebellion against the government of the United States, or who shall in any way give aid or comfort thereto, escaping from such persons and taking refuge within the lines of the

army; and all slaves captured from such persons
or deserted by them and coming under the control of the government of the United States; and
all slaves of such persons found on (or) being
within any place occupied by rebel forces and
afterwards occupied by the forces of the United
States, shall be deemed captives of war, and shall
be forever free of their servitude and not again
held as slaves.[1]

Lincoln's Springfield Farewell Speech

MY FRIENDS: NO ONE, not in my situation, can appreciate my feeling of sadness at this parting. To this place, and the kindness of these people, I owe everything. Here I have lived a quarter of a century, and have passed from a young to an old man. Here my children have been born, and one is buried. I now leave, not knowing when or whether ever I may return, with a task before me greater than that which rested upon [George] Washington. Without the assistance of that Divine Being who ever attended him, I cannot succeed. With that assistance, I cannot fail. Trusting in him who can go with me, and remain with you, and be everywhere for good, let us confidently hope that all will yet be well. To his care commending you, as I hope in your prayers you will commend me, I bid you an affectionate farewell.[1]

Notes

Quotes that are generally accepted by scholars as having
originated with Lincoln but which have no written
backup are listed as "quote attributed to Lincoln."

CHAPTER 1: LEADERSHIP

1. John G. Nicolay and John Hay, eds., *Complete Works of Lincoln* (hereafter NH), 12 vols. (New York: Francis D. Tandy, 1905), 10:65 (April 4, 1864).
2. Michael Burlingame, *An Oral History of Abraham Lincoln: John G. Nicolay's Interviews and Essays* (Carbondale: Southern Illinois University Press, 1996), 54–55 (quote attributed to Lincoln).
3. Harry E. Pratt, *Concerning Mr. Lincoln* (Springfield, IL: Abraham Lincoln Association, 1944), 52 (quote attributed to Lincoln).
4. NH, 6:184–85 (March 4, 1861).
5. NH, 5:327–28 (February 27, 1860).
6. NH, 10:68 (April 4, 1864).
7. William H. Herndon and Jesse W. Weik, *Herndon's Lincoln: The True Story of a Great Life* (Chicago: Belford, Clarke, and Co., 1889), 537.
8. Roy P. Basler, *Collected Works of Abraham Lincoln*, 9 vols.

(New Brunswick, NJ: Rutgers University Press, 1953–55),
2:547 (August 17, 1858).

9. NH, 7:52 (December 3, 1861).

10. Basler, *Collected Works of Lincoln*, 4:149 (December 10,
1860).

11. NH, 10:66 (April 4, 1864).

12. Basler, *Collected Works of Lincoln*, 3:360.

13. Allen T. Rice, *Reminiscences of Abraham Lincoln by Dis-
tinguished Men of His Time* (New York: North American
Review, 1888), 577.

14. F. B. Carpenter, *The Inner Life of Abraham Lincoln*
(Boston: Houghton, Mifflin & Co., 1883), 258–59 (quote
attributed to Lincoln).

15. Rice, *Reminiscences of Lincoln*, 493.

16. NH, 1:14–15.

17. Basler, *Collected Works of Lincoln*, 4:121.

18. Rice, *Reminiscences of Lincoln*, 365.

19. NH, 1:46 (January 2, 1837).

CHAPTER 2: HONESTY

1. Herndon and Weik, *Herndon's Lincoln*, 606.

2. NH, 3:170 (July 17, 1858).

3. NH, 4:113 (September 18, 1858).

4. NH, 1:89 (April 1, 1838).

5. NH, 2:143 (July 1, 1850).

6. Benjamin Thomas, *Abraham Lincoln* (New York: Knopf,
1952), 182 (quote attributed to Lincoln).

7. NH, 2:28 (June 20, 1848).

8. NH, 4:190–91 (September 18, 1858).

9. NH, 4:376 (October 13, 1858).

10. NH, 4:51 (July 15, 1858).

11. J. Turner and L. Turner, *Mary Todd Lincoln: Her Life and Letters* (New York: Knopf, 1972), 180.

12. Burlingame, *Oral History of Lincoln*, 96.

13. Herndon and Weik, *Herndon's Lincoln*, 400 (quote attributed to Lincoln).

14. NH, 2:243 (October 16, 1854).

15. NH, 3:336 (August 27, 1858).

16. Herndon and Weik, *Herndon's Lincoln*, 346 (quote attributed to Lincoln).

17. Douglas Wilson and Rodney Davis, eds., *Herndon's Informants: Letters, Interviews, and Statements About Abraham Lincoln* (Urbana: University of Illinois Press, 1998), 386.

18. NH, 10:158 (July 4, 1864).

19. Emanuel Hertz, *Abraham Lincoln: A New Portrait*, 2 vols. (New York: Liveright, 1931), 2:530 (February 8, 1842) (quote attributed to Lincoln).

20. Alonzo Rothschild, *Honest Abe: A Study in Integrity Based on the Early Life of Abraham Lincoln* (New York: Houghton-Mifflin, 1917), 64.

21. Rice, *Reminiscences of Lincoln*, 575.

22. NH, 1:1–9.

CHAPTER 3: FAITH

1. NH, 8:33 (September 13, 1862).

2. NH, 8:52–53 (September 30, 1862).

3. NH, 10:149 (July 7, 1864).

4. Basler, *Collected Works of Lincoln*, 3:204.

5. Ibid., 6:536 (October 24, 1863).

6. Carpenter, *Inner Life of Lincoln*, 282 (quote attributed to Lincoln).

7. Herndon and Weik, *Herndon's Lincoln*, 359.

8. Joshua Speed, *Reminiscences of Abraham Lincoln and Notes of a Visit to California* (Louisville, KY: John P. Morgan and Co., 1884), 32–33 (quote attributed to Lincoln).

9. Herndon and Weik, *Herndon's Lincoln*, 538.

10. Basler, *Collected Works of Lincoln*, 1:383.

11. NH, 8:50–51 (October 26, 1862).

12. NH, 2:280–281 (August 15, 1855).

13. Salmon P. Chase, *Inside Lincoln's Cabinet: The Civil War Diaries of Salmon P. Chase*, ed. David Donald (New York: Longmans, Green, 1954), 149–50 (quote attributed to Lincoln).

14. NH,10:215–216 (September 4, 1864).

15. NH,8:174 (January 5, 1863).

16. NH,8:235–37 (March 30, 1863) (probably coauthored with the secretary of state, William H. Seward).

17. Carpenter, *Inner Life of Lincoln*, 188 (quote attributed to Lincoln).

18. NH,10:218 (September 7, 1864).

19. Basler, *Collected Works of Lincoln*, 7:170.

Chapter 4: The People

1. Hertz, *Lincoln*, 2:793 (November 21, 1860) (quote attributed to Lincoln).

2. NH,6:312 (July 4, 1861).

3. NH,6:183 (March 4, 1861).

4. NH,6:112 (February 11, 1861).

5. NH,2:69 (July 27, 1848).

6. NH,1:36–37 (January 27, 1838).

7. NH,6:321 (July 4, 1861).

8. NH,7:30 (December 3, 1861).

9. Wilson and Davis, *Herndon's Informants*, 182.

10. NH,6:130 (February 15, 1861).

11. NH,6:123 (February 14, 1861).

12. NH,6:184 (March 4, 1861).

13. NH,6:143 (February 19, 1861).

14. Wilson and Davis, *Herndon's Informants*, 592.

15. Waldo Braden, ed., *Building the Myth: Selected Speeches Memorializing Abraham Lincoln* (Urbana: University of Illinois Press, 1990), 101–2.

16. Hertz, *Lincoln*, 2:806 (February 11, 1861) (quote attributed to Lincoln).

17. NH,6:134 (February 16, 1861).

18. Hertz, *Lincoln*, 2:805 (February 11, 1861) (quote attributed to Lincoln).

19. NH,1:26 (January 11, 1837).

20. Basler, *Collected Works of Lincoln*, 8:138.

21. NH,5:232 (September 17, 1859).

22. Paul Angle, *Abraham Lincoln by Some Men Who Knew Him* (Chicago: Americana House, 1950), 24–25.

23. NH,8:157 (December 31, 1862).

24. NH,6:121 (February 13, 1861).

25. NH,6:141–42.

26. Basler, *Collected Works of Lincoln*, 6:88.

CHAPTER 5: KINDNESS

1. NH,7:293 (July 26, 1862).
2. NH,7:298 (July 28, 1862).
3. NH,7:303 (August 4, 1862).
4. Rice, *Reminiscences of Lincoln*, 338–39.
5. Carpenter, *Inner Life of Lincoln*, 203.
6. NH,10:263–64 (November 10, 1864).
7. Speed, *Reminiscences*, 39 (quote attributed to Lincoln).
8. NH,6:185 (March 4, 1861).
9. NH,11:ix.
10. Emanuel Hertz, *The Hidden Lincoln: From the Letters and Papers of William H. Herndon* (New York: Viking Press, 1938), 327 (quote attributed to Lincoln).
11. Herndon and Weik, *Herndon's Lincoln*, 535.
12. NH,6:72 (November 20, 1860).
13. NH,10:262 (November 8, 1864).
14. Dorothy Lamon, ed., *Recollections of Abraham Lincoln 1847–1865 by Ward Hill Lamon* (Chicago: A. C. McClurg and Co., 1895), 87 (quote attributed to Lincoln).
15. Rice, *Reminiscences of Lincoln*, 338.
16. Basler, *Collected Works of Lincoln*, 7:282.
17. NH,10:208.

CHAPTER 6: LIBERTY

1. NH,5:94 (November 19, 1858).
2. NH,5:61 (October 15, 1858).
3. NH,5:126 (April 6, 1859).
4. NH,11:110 (September 11, 1858).

5. NH,10:77 (April 18, 1864).

6. Basler, *Collected Works of Lincoln*, 3:327.

7. NH,1:49–50 (January 27, 1838).

8. Basler, *Collected Works of Lincoln*, 4:169 (January 1861).

9. Rice, *Reminiscences of Lincoln*, 210.

10. NH,5:361 (March 6, 1860).

11. NH,1:42–43 (January 27, 1838).

12. NH,2:287 (August 24, 1855).

13. Rice, *Reminiscences of Lincoln*, 193–95.

14. NH,2:184 (July 1, 1854).

15. NH,3:51 (July 10, 1858).

16. NH,5:65.

17. NH,9:xiv.

18. NH,1:36 (January 27, 1837).

19. Braden, *Building the Myth*, 99.

CHAPTER 7: COMMON SENSE

1. Basler, *Collected Works of Lincoln*, 4:184 (February 4, 1861).

2. NH,5:190 (September 17, 1859).

3. NH,11:54 (March 15, 1865).

4. Tyler Dennett, ed., *Lincoln and the Civil War in the Diaries and Letters of John Hay* (New York: Dodd, Meade, and Co., 1939), 143 (December 23, 1863) (quote attributed to Lincoln).

5. Carpenter, *Inner Life of Lincoln*, 312–13.

6. Rice, *Reminiscences of Lincoln*, 427.

7. NH,1:2 (March 9, 1832).

8. NH,2:125 (July 13, 1849).

9. NH,7:245 (June 30, 1862).

10. Basler, *Collected Works of Lincoln*, 6:538 (October 26, 1863).

11. John G. Nicolay and John Hay, *Abraham Lincoln: A History*, 10 vols. (New York: Century Co., 1904), 10:377.

12. NH,6:184.

13. NH,2:142.

14. NH,1:197 (February 22, 1842).

15. NH,11:87 (April 11, 1865).

16. Braden, *Building the Myth*, 142.

17. Basler, *Collected Works of Lincoln*, 2:437 (April 6, 1858).

18. Rice, *Reminiscences of Lincoln*, 427–28 (quote attributed to Lincoln).

19. Basler, *Collected Works of Lincoln*, 4:270 (March 4, 1861).

20. Braden, *Building the Myth*, 98.

21. Hertz, *Hidden Lincoln*, 406 (quote attributed to Lincoln).

22. NH,11:85 (April 11, 1865).

CHAPTER 8: CHARACTER

1. Don Fehrenbacher and Virginia Fehrenbacher, eds., *Recollected Words of Abraham Lincoln* (Stanford, CA: Stanford University Press, 1996), 43 (quote attributed to Lincoln).

2. NH,2:192 (October 16, 1854).

3. Basler, *Collected Works of Lincoln*, 7:383 (June 9, 1864).

4. NH,9:199 (November 2, 1863).

5. Basler, *Collected Works of Lincoln*, 7:507 (August 19, 1864).

6. NH,1:56 (August 16, 1837).

7. Wilson and Davis, *Herndon's Informants*, 499.

8. NH,1:137 (December 20, 1839).

9. NH,8:69 (October 27, 1862).

10. Rice, *Reminiscences of Lincoln*, 575–76.

11. Herndon and Weik, *Herndon's Lincoln*, 531 (quote attributed to Lincoln).

12. Basler, *Collected Works of Lincoln*, 3:436 (September 16, 1859).

13. Braden, *Building the Myth*, 118.

14. NH,7:304 (August 6, 1862).

15. Michael Burlingame, ed., *Lincoln Observed: The Civil War Dispatches of Noah Brooks* (Baltimore: Johns Hopkins University Press, 1998), 211 (quote attributed to Lincoln).

16. NH,1:53 (May 7, 1837).

17. Carl Sandburg, *Abraham Lincoln: The War Years*, 6 vols. (New York: Scribner's, 1939), 3:559 (quote attributed to Lincoln).

18. NH,11:92 (April 11, 1865).

19. NH,7:159.

20. NH,5:xxix.

Chapter 9: Democracy

1. Basler, *Collected Works of Lincoln*, 2:385 (December 10, 1856).

2. NH,6:157 (February 22, 1861).

3. Dennett, *Lincoln and the Civil War*, 19–20 (quote attributed to Lincoln).

4. NH,6:151–52 (February 21, 1861).

5. NH,2:184 (July 1, 1854).

6. NH,2:186–87 (July 1, 1854).

7. NH,5:ix.

8. NH,3:252 (August 21, 1858).

9. NH,2:226–27 (October 16, 1854).

10. NH,1:14 (June 13, 1836).

11. Basler, *Collected Works of Lincoln*, 2:532 (August 1, 1858).

12. Braden, *Building the Myth*, 101–2.

13. NH,6:304 (July 4, 1861).

14. NH,1:42 (January 27, 1838).

15. NH,2:165 (July 6, 1852).

16. NH,2:37 (June 20, 1848).

17. NH,4:226 (December 28, 1857).

18. NH,2:235 (October 16, 1854).

19. Basler, *Collected Works of Lincoln*, 4:197 (February 12, 1861).

20. Ibid., 4:168–69.

21. NH,3:1–2.

Chapter 10: Perseverance

1. Basler, *Collected Works of Lincoln*, 2:327 (November 5, 1855).

2. Ibid., 4:87 (July 22, 1860).

3. NH,1:138 (December 26, 1839).

4. Basler, *Collected Works of Lincoln*, 3:90 (September 6, 1858).

5. NH,7:240 (June 29, 1862).

6. Wilson and Davis, *Herndon's Informants*, 113.

7. NH,2:57 (July 10, 1848).

8. NH,1:7 (March 9, 1832).

9. Braden, *Building the Myth*, 155.

10. Basler, *Collected Works of Lincoln*, 7:495 (August 15, 1864).

11. NH,2:46 (June 20, 1848).

12. NH,1:314 (December 1, 1847).

13. NH,3:15 (June 16, 1858).

14. Basler, *Collected Works of Lincoln*, 1:489 (July 20, 1848).

15. Ibid., 5:288 (June 28, 1862).

16. H. S. Krans, *The Lincoln Tribute Book* (New York: Putnam's, 1909), 22.

17. Ida M. Tarbell and J. M. Davis, *The Early Life of Abraham Lincoln* (New York: McClure, 1896), 62 (quote attributed to Lincoln).

18. NH,6:59 (September 25, 1860).

19. Herndon and Weik, *Herndon's Lincoln*, 375.

20. NH,2:150 (November 4, 1851).

21. NH,10:202–3 (August 22, 1864).

22. Wilson and Davis, *Herndon's Informants*, 360.

23. NH,8:288.

Chapter 11: Humor

1. Fehrenbacher and Fehrenbacher, *Recollected Words of Lincoln*, 340 (quote attributed to Lincoln).

2. William H. Herndon, "An Analysis of the Character of Abraham Lincoln," *Abraham Lincoln Quarterly* 1 (1940–41): 420 (quote attributed to Lincoln).

3. NH,2:88 (July 27, 1848).

4. NH,1:92 (April 1, 1838).

5. Angle, *Lincoln*, 51 (quote attributed to Lincoln).

6. NH,1:27 (January 11, 1837).

7. P. M. Zall, ed., *Abe Lincoln Laughing* (Berkeley and Los Angeles: University of California Press, 1982), 5.

8. NH,5:125 (April 6, 1859).

9. Basler, *Collected Works of Lincoln*, 3:20 (August 21, 1858).

10. NH,1:92 (April 1, 1838).

11. NH,2:83 (July 27, 1848).

12. Basler, *Collected Works of Lincoln*, 5:22 (November 13, 1861).

13. Ibid., 3:279 (October 13, 1858).

14. Ibid., 2:330 (February 13, 1856).

15. Emanuel Hertz, *Lincoln Talks* (New York: Viking, 1939), 459 (quote attributed to Lincoln).

16. Rice, *Reminiscences of Lincoln*, 388.

17. Basler, *Collected Works of Lincoln*, 1:485 (June 20, 1848).

18. Ibid., 2:552 (August 21, 1858).

19. Zall, *Lincoln Laughing*, 48 (quote attributed to Lincoln).

Chapter 12: Hope

1. NH,2:248 (October 16, 1854).

2. NH,9:102 (May 26, 1863).

3. Basler, *Collected Works of Lincoln*, 2:89 (July 25, 1850).

4. NH,10:209 (August 31, 1864).

5. NH,8:5 (August 14, 1862).

6. NH,2:47 (March 4, 1865).

7. NH,8:131 (December 1, 1862).

8. NH,7:60 (December 3, 1861).

9. NH,2:185 (July 1, 1854).

10. Braden, *Building the Myth*, 167.

11. Ibid., 154.

12. NH,2:241 (October 16, 1854).

13. Basler, *Collected Works of Lincoln*, 2:364 (August 27, 1856).

14. NH,6:136 (February 16, 1861).

15. NH,2:184 (July 1, 1854).

16. NH,6:157 (February 22, 1861).

THE GETTYSBURG ADDRESS

1. NH,9:209–10 (November 19, 1863).

EXCERPT FROM LINCOLN'S FIRST INAUGURAL ADDRESS

1. NH,6:173–75 (March 4, 1861).

LINCOLN'S SECOND INAUGURAL ADDRESS

1. NH,2:44–47 (March 4, 1865).

FIRST ANNUAL THANKSGIVING DAY PROCLAMATION

1. NH,9:151–53 (October 3, 1863).

EXCERPT FROM LINCOLN'S FIRST ADDRESS TO CONGRESS

1. NH,6:322–25 (July 4, 1861).

EXCERPT FROM THE EMANCIPATION PROCLAMATION

1. NH,8:37 (September 22, 1862).

LINCOLN'S SPRINGFIELD FAREWELL SPEECH

1. NH,6:110–11 (February 11, 1861).

About the Author

GORDON LEIDNER has been a lifelong student
of Abraham Lincoln and the American Civil War.
He has authored three books on Abraham Lincoln,
numerous articles, and maintains the popular
history Web site www.greatamericanhistory.net.
He is a board member of the Abraham Lincoln
Institute, and lives near Annapolis, Maryland,
with Jean, his wife of thirty years.